*I did not come here
for [religious] reasons. I came here
to take away their gold.*

Francisco Pizarro, when pressed
by a missionary to instruct the
Inca in the Christian faith

This book is for Lisa, Joe, and Mali.

Photographs © 2009: akg-Images, London: 87 top; AP Images/Martin Mejia: 63; Art Resource, NY/ Bildarchiv Preussischer Kulturbesitz: 25, 44, 87 bottom, 117; Bridgeman Art Library International Ltd., London/New York: 85, 98 (Bibliotheque Nationale, Paris, France/Lauros/Giraudon), 91 top left, 113 (British Museum, London, UK); Corbis Images: 17, 86 top right (Stefano Amantini/Atlantide Phototravel), 86 top left (Stefano Bianchetti), 89 left (Tim Davis), 82 (Theodor de Bry/Bettmann), 38 (J.L. Kraemer/Blue Lantern Studio), 53 (Hugh Sitton/zefa), 100 (The Gallery Collection); Getty Images/Robert Harding: 61; North Wind Picture Archives: 48, 49, 70, 89 right, 108; Superstock, Inc./age fotostock: 88 bottom; The Art Archive/Picture Desk: 97 (Gianni Dagli Orti/Biblioteca Nacional, Madrid), 102, 120 (Gianni Dagli Orti/Biblioteca Nazionale Marciana, Venice), 19 (Alfredo Dagli Orti/Bibliotheque des Arts Decoratifs, Paris), 75 (Mireille Vautier); Archives/The Florida Museum of Natural History: 91 bottom; The Granger Collection, New York: 10, 21, 23, 28, 30, 41, 78, 86 bottom, 88 center, 88 top, 90 top, 91 top right; The Image Works: 66 (ARPL/HIP), 81, 90 bottom (Topham).

Illustrations by XNR Productions, Inc.: 4, 5, 8, 9
Cover art, page 8 inset by Mark Summers
Chapter art by Raphael Montoliu

Library of Congress Cataloging-in-Publication Data

DiConsiglio, John.
Francisco Pizarro : destroyer of the Inca Empire / John DiConsiglio.
p. cm. — (A wicked history)
Includes bibliographical references and index.
ISBN-13: 978-0-531-18551-3 (lib. bdg.) 978-0-531-22172-3 (pbk.)
ISBN-10: 0-531-18551-6 (lib. bdg.)   0-531-22172-5 (pbk.)
1. Pizarro, Francisco, ca. 1475-1541—Juvenile literature. 2.
Peru—History—Conquest, 1522-1548—Juvenile literature. 3.
Conquerors—Peru—Biography—Juvenile literature. 4.
Conquerors—Spain—Biography—Juvenile literature. 5.
Explorers—Peru—Biography—Juvenile literature. 6.
Explorers—Spain—Biography—Juvenile literature. I. Title.
F3442.P776D54 2009
985'.02092—dc22
[B]

2008010819

Tod Olson, Series Editor
Marie O'Neill, Art Director
Allicette Torres, Cover Design
SimonSays Design!, Book Design and Production

© 2009 Scholastic Inc.

All rights reserved. Published by Franklin Watts, an imprint of Scholastic Inc.
Published simultaneously in Canada. Printed in the United States of America.

1 2 3 4 5 6 7 8 9 10 R 18 17 16 15 14 13 12 11 10 09   23

Francisco Pizarro

Destroyer of the Inca Empire

JOHN DICONSIGLIO

Franklin Watts ®
An Imprint of Scholastic Inc.
New York   Toronto   London   Auckland   Sydney
Mexico City   New Delhi   Hong Kong
Danbury, Connecticut

The World of Francisco Pizarro

In the 16th century, Pizarro and others explored the Western Hemisphere—and wiped out millions of the people who lived there.

NORTH AMERICA

Tenochtitlán

CUBA

HISPANIOLA

Caribbean Sea

Atlantic Ocean

Gulf of Urabá

Panama — Turbaco

D

San Sebastián

Santa María la Antigua del Darién

San Juan River

Gallo Island

Gulf of Guayaquil

E Tumbes

Tangarara — Cajas

F Cajamarca

Amazon — *River*

Pacific Ocean

Lima **H**

Cuzco

G

Las Salinas

Mount Ampato ▲

Andes Mts.

SOUTH AMERICA

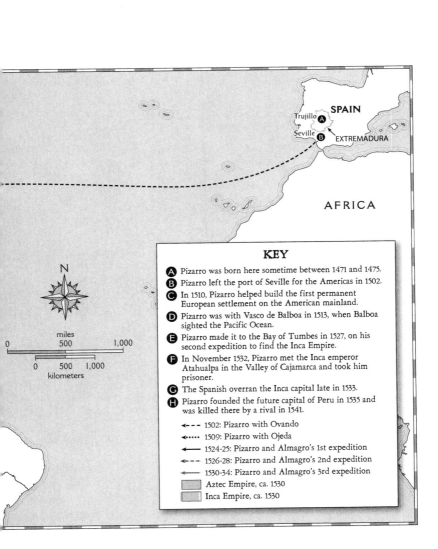

SPAIN

Trujillo **A**

Seville **B**

EXTREMADURA

AFRICA

KEY

A Pizarro was born here sometime between 1471 and 1475.

B Pizarro left the port of Seville for the Americas in 1502.

C In 1510, Pizarro helped build the first permanent European settlement on the American mainland.

D Pizarro was with Vasco de Balboa in 1513, when Balboa sighted the Pacific Ocean.

E Pizarro made it to the Bay of Tumbes in 1527, on his second expedition to find the Inca Empire.

F In November 1532, Pizarro met the Inca emperor Atahualpa in the Valley of Cajamarca and took him prisoner.

G The Spanish overran the Inca capital late in 1533.

H Pizarro founded the future capital of Peru in 1535 and was killed there by a rival in 1541.

◄--- 1502: Pizarro with Ovando

◄···· 1509: Pizarro with Ojeda

◄— 1524-25: Pizarro and Almagro's 1st expedition

◄-◄- 1526-28: Pizarro and Almagro's 2nd expedition

◄— 1530-34: Pizarro and Almagro's 3rd expedition

Aztec Empire, ca. 1530

Inca Empire, ca. 1530

N

miles
0   500   1,000

0   500   1,000
kilometers

TABLE OF CONTENTS

A Wicked Web

A look at the allies and enemies of Francisco Pizarro.

In Spain

〜〜〜〜〜〜〜〜〜〜〜

GONZALO "THE TALL" PIZARRO ——— FRANCISCA GONZALEZ
Francisco's father; an officer in the   Francisco's mother
Spanish army

FERDINAND II ——— ISABELLA I
king of Spain, 1479–1516   queen of Spain, 1474–1504

CHARLES V
Holy Roman Emperor from 1519–1556;
king of Spain (as Charles I)
from 1516–1556;
grandson of Ferdinand II

In America

〜〜〜〜〜〜〜〜〜〜〜〜〜

THE INCA

HUAYNA CAPAC
Inca emperor at time of Pizarro's
first arrival in Peru

FRANCISCO PIZARRO

ATAHUALPA
son of Huayna Capac; last
independent ruler of Inca Empire

TUPAC HUALLPA
half brother of Huascar; named
emperor by Pizarro after
Atahualpa's execution

HUASCAR
half brother of Atahualpa; killed
in civil war over succession

MANCO
half brother of Tupac Huallpa;
succeeded him as emperor

In America

꙾꙾꙾꙾꙾꙾꙾꙾꙾꙾꙾

SPANIARDS

NICOLÁS DE OVANDO
governor of Hispaniola and
commander of Pizarro's first
expedition to America

ALONSO DE OJEDA
captain of Pizarro's first voyage
to the mainland and founder of
first Spanish settlement there

MARTÍN DE ENCISO
Ojeda's partner and founder of
Santa María, first Spanish
settlement in present-day Panama

VASCO DE BALBOA
rival of Enciso for governorship
of Darién; led Pizarro and others
to Pacific Ocean

PEDRO ARIAS DE ÁVILA
(PEDRARIAS)
replaced Balboa as governor and
had him executed for treason

HERNÁN CORTÉS
distant cousin of Pizarro;
conqueror of the Aztecs

DIEGO DE ALMAGRO
Pizarro's partner and eventual
rival in the quest for Peru

HERNANDO DE SOTO
Spanish explorer who
accompanied Pizarro to Peru

DIEGO DE ALMAGRO
THE YOUNGER
son of Diego de Almagro;
avenged the death of his father
by having Pizarro killed

HERNANDO, JUAN, AND
GONZALO PIZARRO
Francisco's half brothers and
partners in the quest for Peru

BARTOLOMÉ RUIZ
navigator on second expedition
to Peru; first to see the Inca

FRIAR VICENTE
first Spanish bishop of Peru and
chronicler of the conquest

FRANCISCO PIZARRO, c. 1471–1541

To HIS SUBJECTS, EMPEROR ATAHUALPA was a god. He was the leader of the great Inca Empire, and his kingdom stretched more than 2,500 miles down the west coast of South America. Some 12 million people from the northern border of what is now Ecuador to central Chile owed allegiance to Atahualpa.

But in November 1532, this mighty lord was a prisoner, begging for his life. An invading army of a few hundred Spaniards had stormed Atahualpa's royal city high in the Andes Mountains. They had slaughtered thousands of Inca warriors and looted the city. Now the Inca emperor sat shackled in a stone house, guarded by Spanish soldiers.

Shortly after Atahualpa's capture, the leader of the Spaniards appeared at his prisoner's door. The soldier's name was Francisco Pizarro. He was about 60 years old—an unusually old man for such a dangerous profession. He was tall and soft-spoken, but hardened by years of rugged adventure.

For more than half his life, Pizarro had led small bands of ragged Spanish soldiers through the jungles of the New World with one main purpose in mind— to find gold. He had conquered tribes of native people. He had won new lands for Spain and sent treasure home to his king. But the great stashes of gold that supposedly lay hidden in the jungle had eluded him—until now.

In the stone cell, Pizarro faced his prisoner and demanded that Atahualpa bring him great riches. Atahualpa spoke through an interpreter. He stood and stretched his arm high up the prison wall. "Tell the Christians," he said, "that if they do not kill me I will give them this entire chamber filled with gold." When Pizarro merely raised his eyebrow, Atahualpa continued. Spare his life, and he would fill the room with gold—and twice more with silver.

Finally, Pizarro agreed, and the Inca emperor sent messengers to collect gold from the far corners of his empire. But Pizarro knew he was in a dangerous position. Atahualpa's chiefs commanded three separate armies that lay within a couple of weeks' march. At any moment, the Inca emperor could bring as many as 100,000 warriors to his aid. Pizarro had only 200 soldiers to fend them off. Reinforcements were on their way but wouldn't arrive for several months.

Pizarro settled in to wait. He hoped that with their leader in prison the entire Inca Empire would be paralyzed. Tribes conquered by the Inca could be convinced to rise up against their Inca masters. That was Pizarro's plan. If it succeeded, he would win fabulous riches for himself and for Spain, and destroy the mightiest empire in the New World. If it failed, he and his men would die in bloody combat, far from their homelands in Spain.

PART 1

The Young Conquistador

CHAPTER 1

A Soldier's Life

A lowly pig farmer seeks
FAME AND FORTUNE
IN BATTLE.

THE STORY OF FRANCISCO PIZARRO BEGINS in a dusty Spanish town called Trujillo, a six-month ocean voyage from Peru. Trujillo is located in the province of Extremadura. *Extremadura* comes from a Latin word meaning "remote and harsh," and the area lives up to its name. The dry, dusty province is tormented by blazing heat in the summer and bitter cold in the winter. In Pizarro's day, Extremaduran men tended to be rugged and independent. They worked

LEGEND HAS IT that Francisco Pizarro was abandoned by his mother on the steps of the Church of Santa Maria in Trujillo, Spain.

as farmers struggling to grow crops in the sandy soil. They often plucked lizards from the dirt for food.

Pizarro was born sometime between 1471 and 1475. His father, the soldier Gonzalo Pizarro, was nicknamed "Pizarro the Tall." As a captain in the Spanish army, Gonzalo had fought wars throughout Europe. On one trip home, he met Francisca Gonzalez, a humble washerwoman. The couple never married, even after Francisco was born. Some stories say Francisca abandoned the baby on the doorstep of Extremadura's Church of Santa Maria.

17

Young Francisco's grandparents probably took him in. Like many young people in Extremadura, Francisco didn't go to school. Throughout his life, he never learned to read or write.

When Francisco was a teenager, he and his mother most likely moved to Seville, in southern Spain. There, Pizarro made a living as a pig farmer. His future did not look bright. His father was of noble birth, but as an illegitimate child, Francisco had no right to his father's title or property. In Seville, he had little hope of finding adventure or wealth. So, in the 1490s, he joined the army.

As a soldier, young Pizarro became a member of one of Europe's most feared fighting forces. Spanish archers used deadly crossbows that fired arrows known as bolts. Expert archers could shoot a bolt through steel armor at a distance of a hundred yards. Foot soldiers used an early form of musket known as a harquebus. These weapons were slow to load and hard to aim, but they were a fearsome sight on the battlefield. Spanish

PIZARRO TRAINED TO BE A SOLDIER in the Spanish army.
The soldiers to the left have crossbows, capable of piercing steel. The
others have lances, used for stabbing people from horseback.

foot soldiers were supported by a cavalry force whose horsemen ranked among the best in Europe. They led the army into battle with swords and 14-foot lances.

In addition to his training on the battlefield, Pizarro would have become practiced at the art of looting. Spanish soldiers weren't paid by their commanders. They earned their pay by stealing from the people they conquered. It was a tactic Pizarro would eventually use on an enormous scale.

COLUMBUS IN THE NEW WORLD

AS PIZARRO WAS LEARNING THE ART OF BATTLE, an explorer named Christopher Columbus was preparing for a mission that would change history. On August 3, 1492, Columbus left Spain and headed west across the Atlantic Ocean, hoping to find a sea route to Asia.

Instead, Columbus landed on Hispaniola, an island in the Caribbean Sea that is now the Dominican Republic and Haiti. He was met by members of the local Taíno tribe. Thinking he had arrived in a group of Asian islands known as the Indies, Columbus called the Taínos "Indians."

Columbus sailed back to Spain and told King Ferdinand and Queen Isabella about this New World. They ordered him to return, claim land for Spain, bring back treasure, and convert the Indians "to our Holy Catholic Faith."

Columbus returned to Hispaniola and set up the first Spanish settlement in the New World. He brought 1,500 armed soldiers as well as attack dogs—and immediately ordered the Taínos to collect gold, cotton, and food.

The conquest of the Americas had begun.

TAÍNOS FLEE from Columbus as he approaches their island in 1492. Believing he had reached the West Indies, he called the Taínos "Indians."

Chapter 2

ഹഹഹഹഹഹഹഹഹഹ

To the New World

Pizarro leaves Spain behind in search
of ADVENTURE OVERSEAS.

AFTER SERVING IN THE MILITARY, PIZARRO
returned to Seville. There he may have encountered
soldiers returning from the New World. These
conquistadors—or conquerors—often bragged about
the great riches to be found across the ocean.

In 1502, Pizarro found a job on the largest fleet of
ships yet to leave Spain for the New World. Thirty
ships set sail on February 13, carrying 2,500 passengers.
On board was Nicolás de Ovando, who had just been
named governor of Hispaniola by King Ferdinand and

CARAVELS WERE THE FASTEST SHIPS of the time. They also could make long voyages, so they were used on expeditions to the New World.

Queen Isabella. Governor Ovando's mission was to turn the island into a profitable colony for Spain.

In the early 1500s, the journey across the Atlantic was grueling. Pizarro probably sailed in a caravel, a 100-foot wooden ship with two or three masts. Passengers aboard these ships faced a constant battle against disease, rot, and vermin. Water seeped through the hold. Foul odors drifted through the air—sweat, rotting wood, spoiled food, and the stench of horses brought on the journey. Rats and mice scurried freely through the ship. Food was contaminated with weevils, urine, and rodent dung.

The crowded ships offered no privacy. Sailors strung hammocks anywhere they could, sleeping in the middle of decks and halls. Even going to the bathroom was an adventure. A sailor usually balanced on the rail of the ship and eased down into a seat called a *jardine* (named after a flower). There was always the danger that he would fall through the jardine into the waves below.

Pizarro survived the trip and aided in Governor Ovando's efforts to exploit Hispaniola. Ovando started large plantations. He opened new gold and silver mines. He also brought the first Africans to the Americas—forcing them to work as slaves in the fields and the mines.

The governor also enslaved the Taínos. Under Queen Isabella's orders, the native people were to be converted to Christianity, not put to work. But Hispaniola lay beyond the queen's reach. And as long

THE SPANISH ENSLAVED the native people of Hispaniola. They also brought Africans to the island to work as slaves.

as Ovando sent part of the settlement's wealth back to Spain, he was mostly free to rule as he wanted. In a few years, the once independent Taínos were nearly wiped out by overwork, disease, and war. Between 1492 and 1507, the native population dropped from 500,000 to 60,000.

It's not clear what role Pizarro played in Governor Ovando's colony. For seven years there's no sign of Pizarro in any historical documents. But in 1509, he appears again, headed for an encounter with the Indians of South America.

A CONTINENT OF GOLD?

BY 1509, THE SPANISH HAD COLONIZED THE larger islands in the Caribbean Sea. But little was known about the huge continent that's now known as South America.

Many people believed that the continent was full of gold. In 1502, Columbus had landed in what is now Panama. After listening to the tales of the local tribes, he named the region *Castilla del Oro*, or Castle of Gold.

Soon after, private adventurers made expeditions along the coast of South America. The native people they met often told them stories about nearby kingdoms of gold.

For conquistadors like Pizarro, this vast continent seemed to offer riches beyond their wildest imaginings.

RUMORS OF GOLD lured Pizarro from Hispaniola to the South American mainland.

CHAPTER 3

Claiming a Continent

POISON ARROWS greet Pizarro on his first voyage to the mainland.

ON NOVEMBER 12, 1509, PIZARRO LEFT Hispaniola on a 500-mile voyage south to the mainland of what is now called South America. This time, he sailed under the command of Alonso de Ojeda. Ojeda had a fleet of four ships, 300 men, and a dozen horses. And he had orders from King Ferdinand and Queen Isabella to start the first Spanish colony on the mainland.

SPANISH LAW REQUIRED the conquistadors to offer peace to Indians who accepted Christianity. Ojeda's priest read the offer in Latin, a language the Indians couldn't possibly understand.

Pizarro must have been eager with anticipation. He most certainly had heard rumors about the huge continent with kingdoms full of gold and other riches.

Weeks later, Ojeda and Pizarro landed on the northern coast of what is now Colombia. Ojeda took a small party ashore and found a group of native people waiting for him. The Spaniard immediately had a priest read a long proclamation in Latin. The priest explained that God's representative on earth, the pope, had given the land they stood on to the rulers of Spain. He insisted that the Indians obey their new king, Ferdinand II, and convert to Christianity "of their free and cheerful will." If they agreed, they would be granted "many favors." If they resisted, the Spaniards would take their "wives and children and make slaves of them."

The native people could not have understood a word of this bizarre speech. But with several dozen men in armor facing them with swords and lances, they no doubt got the message. In the confusion that followed, most of the Indians fled. Ojeda's men slaughtered the rest.

Ojeda quickly gathered a small party of soldiers to chase the Indians. He led his men into the jungle—directly into an ambush. Warriors swept in from all sides. Poison-tipped arrows rained down on the Spaniards, sending them fleeing for their lives. Only Ojeda and one other man from his group escaped to the ships.

OJEDA AND HIS MEN BATTLE a group of Indians. The Spaniards used their horses and steel weapons to overpower the native tribes.

Reinforcements arrived within weeks and Ojeda took his revenge, wiping out a local village. Then he sailed southwest along the coast in search of a place to settle. He found it in the Gulf of Urabá. There, Ojeda, Pizarro, and the remaining members of the expedition built a small fort and named it San Sebastian.

Pizarro had made it to the outer edge of European settlement. Laid out before him was the promise of gold and glory. But neither was going to come without a struggle.

CHAPTER 4

Struggle for Survival

TRAPPED INSIDE A TINY FORT, Pizarro takes command.

WITHIN WEEKS, SAN SEBASTIAN BECAME a virtual prison for Ojeda, Pizarro, and the other conquistadors. The local Indians had trapped the Spaniards inside the fort, sending poison arrows whistling over the wooden walls.

Before long, food supplies ran short. Ojeda sailed off to find supplies and reinforcements. He placed Pizarro in command of the settlement and left him with the two smallest of their four boats.

Pizarro now had men looking to him for leadership. And the challenge could not have been greater. The men were surrounded by tribes determined to drive them out. The Spaniards risked their lives any time they left the fort to hunt, fish, or gather food. Eventually, they killed and ate their horses. Tempers no doubt flared as they struggled to stay alive.

Pizarro knew he had to evacuate the settlement. But he had 70 men—too many for the boats Ojeda had left him. Pizarro called his men together and asked for volunteers to stay behind. When no one stepped forward, he settled in to wait.

After several months, disease and Indian attacks had killed off enough soldiers for Pizarro to attempt the voyage. He ordered the remaining men into the boats. They had barely left sight of shore when the waves swamped one of the boats. It floundered in the sea and sank with all its crew.

Pizarro and the other survivors huddled in their small ship, starving and battered by wind and rain. They were drifting north toward Hispaniola when they sighted two tall masts on the horizon. The ships carried Ojeda's partner, Martín de Enciso. Enciso had been appointed the new governor of San Sebastian. He was headed for the settlement with 150 men and fresh supplies.

The crew arrived at San Sebastian to find the settlement completely destroyed. Pizarro warned Enciso about the fierce Indian resistance and pressed him to turn the ships around. But Enciso refused. The argument became so heated that both men reached for their swords. Before they could duel, one of Enciso's soldiers stepped between them. His name was Vasco de Balboa.

Balboa was a charming, well-spoken soldier who came from Pizarro's home region of Extremadura. He had journeyed to Hispaniola to be a farmer. But he gave in to the allure of adventure and wealth. He went on several exploring expeditions and then gambled his way into debt. He had stowed away on Enciso's ship to get away from his creditors.

Balboa suggested a different spot for a settlement— across the Gulf of Urabá in Darién. He had explored the area before, and he assured the other conquistadors that "the Indians there do not use poison arrows."

Hopeful that Balboa was right, the soldiers sailed west to Darién, in present-day Panama. They battled an Indian *cacique*, or chief, and seized his village. There, in September 1510, they founded the settlement of Santa María la Antigua del Darién, the first permanent European settlement on the mainland of America.

Little did they know that just 50 miles to the west lay the Pacific Ocean. Its vast waters would give Pizarro and others access to new lands. Their small settlement would soon become a base for the conquest of a continent.

CHAPTER 5

Behold the Ocean!

Pizarro follows a famous explorer
TO THE MIGHTY PACIFIC.

IN DARIÉN, THE POPULAR BALBOA challenged Governor Enciso for control of the settlement. With Pizarro and many others backing him, Balboa forced Enciso to step down. Balboa named himself governor and appointed Pizarro commander of the troops. Then Balboa sent the enraged Enciso back to Spain, where he spread stories of Balboa's treachery.

Pizarro accompanied Governor Balboa on a series of raids along the coast. He watched the governor both befriend and terrorize local Indians. In some cases,

Balboa backed one warring tribe against another—and shared in the spoils from the war. Other times, he ransacked villages and stole anything of value.

On one of his expeditions, Balboa reached the land of a cacique named Comagre. The cacique's eldest son, Panquiaco, told Balboa of a province where the people were so rich that they ate and drank from golden plates and goblets. To get there, Panquiaco said, Balboa would have to conquer the tribes living by the "other sea."

In the fall of 1513, Balboa and Pizarro left Santa María with almost 200 Spaniards and 1,000 Indian allies in search of this other sea. They hacked their way southwest through the dense jungle, defeating two local tribes along the way. On September 25, Balboa climbed alone to the peak of a mountain. When he reached the top, he saw a great body of water stretching across the horizon to the southwest. Balboa had become the first European to see the eastern rim of the Pacific Ocean.

BALBOA SHOWS HIS MEN the Pacific Ocean. He named it the South
Sea and claimed it—and all the land it touched—for Spain.

The explorer shouted down to his comrades: "Behold the much-desired ocean!" Pizarro and the troops rushed to the top of the mountain to see for themselves.

For the next four days, Balboa and his men continued their trek westward. Finally, they reached the shores of the ocean. Balboa waded waist-deep into the water. He thrust his sword into what he called the "South Sea" and loudly claimed it and all the land it touched for Spain.

But Balboa's joy over his great achievement was short-lived. When the party returned to the settlement, they received word that a new governor would soon arrive to replace Balboa. In July 1514, Pedro Arias de Ávila, known as Pedrarias, arrived with instructions from the king of Spain to take control of Darién. Balboa gave up his post without a fight.

Pizarro seems to have been perfectly happy to switch his allegiance to the new governor. In 1518, acting on orders from Governor Pedrarias, Pizarro took a group of soldiers and intercepted Balboa near the South Sea. Pizarro arrested his former ally and mentor and accused Balboa of trying to start his own colony on the shores of the sea. Pizarro dragged Balboa back to Santa María, where he was tried for treason.

In January 1519, Balboa was beheaded. Governor Pedrarias had the famous explorer's head kept on public display for several days.

Pizarro was rewarded handsomely for siding with Pedrarias. In August 1519, the governor opened a port city on the South Sea and called it Panama. The new city gave Spanish ships access to the entire west coast of the continent. And Francisco Pizarro became its mayor.

CONQUEROR OF THE AZTECS

AS PIZARRO SETTLED IN TO GOVERN PANAMA, a distant cousin of his was on the march 1,400 miles to the northwest. In November 1519, Hernán Cortés and 400 Spanish soldiers arrived in Tenochtitlán, the capital of the Aztec Empire in Mexico. The powerful Aztecs were rich with gold. They were fierce warriors who had conquered tribes throughout Mexico.

Cortés rallied the defeated tribes against the Aztecs. Within two years, he had conquered the Aztecs and destroyed their capital. His men looted temples and burned villages. Anything made of gold was melted down and shipped to Spain.

To conquistadors like Pizarro, the treasure found in Mexico seemed to prove that the rumors were true. The Americas did in fact conceal great kingdoms of gold— and Pizarro was determined to conquer the next one himself.

HERNÁN CORTÉS, Pizarro's cousin, conquered the Aztecs.

C H A P T E R   6

The Partnership

With a deal sealed by a handshake, THE SEARCH FOR PERU BEGINS.

PIZARRO WAS NOW IN HIS LATE FORTIES, an old man for a soldier. He had served under two famous captains—and turned against one of them to please a powerful politician. He was gaining a reputation as a fearless fighter and a fiercely ambitious man.

During his years as mayor of Panama, Pizarro helped transform the colony from a minor outpost to a wildly successful settlement. It soon replaced Santo Domingo in Hispaniola as Spain's most important city in the New World.

But in 1522, Pizarro's attention was diverted. An adventurer returned to Panama and told an exciting tale. He had been part of a group of Spaniards who traveled 600 miles down the western coast of South America. There, they met Indians who told them about a gold-rich land called Peru.

Pizarro heard the story and decided his chance had come. He would set out to find Peru. But the venture was too big for him to handle alone. He needed partners to help recruit soldiers, gather supplies, and raise money.

Diego de Almagro became Pizarro's main partner. Almagro was a conquistador, much like Pizarro himself. He had fought in many battles in the New World. He was said to be a master tracker who could find the smallest traces of his enemy hiding in thick forests. But unlike the tall, tight-lipped Pizarro, the smaller Almagro had a quick tongue and temper. Pizarro's servant described Almagro as "a profane man, foul-mouthed, who, when roused to anger, mistreated those around

PIZARRO AND DIEGO DE ALMAGRO make an agreement to search
for Peru. Their other partner was a priest named Hernando de Luque.
The three agreed to split the profits from their expeditions.

him." Pizarro and Almagro argued often over plans for
the expedition.

Pizarro and Almagro got permission from
Governor Pedrarias to launch their expedition. They
gathered recruits among the soldiers and adventurers
in Panama, and in September 1524, Pizarro set out

down the coast. Using one of Balboa's old boats, he traveled south from Panama with 80 Spanish soldiers, 40 horses, and visions of gold and glory. Almagro followed with another crew shortly after.

This first attempt to find the wealthy land of Peru failed miserably. The journey was plagued by dwindling supplies, stormy seas, snake-infested swamps, and Indian attacks. In one battle, Almagro lost an eye. Pizarro's crew found only a few gold ornaments in a deserted village. Discouraged and tired, they limped back to Panama in 1525, having found no sign of the legendary kingdom of Peru.

A Line in the Sand

DISEASE AND STARVATION nearly wreck the second expedition to find Peru.

Pizarro REFUSED TO GIVE UP THE QUEST for Peru. He and Almagro pleaded with Governor Pedrarias for a second chance. Finally, the governor approved another voyage—in return for a share of their profits.

In August 1526, the partners set sail on their second expedition. This time, they brought two ships, 160 men, and some horses. Pizarro was at least 50 years old. Almagro was older.

Their ships dropped anchor 600 miles south of Panama, off the coast of what is now northern Ecuador.

Pizarro led a landing party ashore. The crew stumbled into a recently abandoned village. They picked through old fishing nets and discarded pots. When they found a few gold trinkets scattered in the dirt, Pizarro became convinced that they were on the right path.

Pizarro put a new plan into action. He stayed with a party of soldiers to explore the coast on foot. He ordered Almagro to take one of the ships back to Panama for supplies. A navigator named Bartolomé Ruiz took command of the other ship. He sailed south to explore new territory.

For three months, Pizarro and his band of soldiers hacked through jungle vines and waded across waist-deep swamps. Poisonous insects and huge snakes plagued them. Worst of all were the clouds of mosquitoes that spread disease with their constant bites.

Ruiz and Almagro finally returned to find Pizarro's party at the mouth of the San Juan River. The soldiers were nearly starved. Their clothes were rags on their bone-thin frames. The men wanted to abandon the mission. But Ruiz's report gave Pizarro hope. Along Ecuador's coast, Ruiz had met Indians traveling in balsa rafts. They told of a powerful king who lived to the south and ruled all the lands for miles.

Pizarro decided they were on the verge of finding

Peru. Again he ordered Almagro back to Panama for supplies. Almagro accused Pizarro of scheming to keep the expedition's loot for himself. But he gave in.

Pizarro and his men retreated to a nearby island. After six months of Indian attacks and starvation, a messenger arrived from Almagro. The news was not good. Pedrarias had been replaced as governor of Panama.

PIZARRO DRAWS A LINE in the sand. He challenges those who have the courage to continue the expedition to move to his side of the line. Thirteen men follow him.

The new governor had no interest in Pizarro's voyage and ordered the expedition to return immediately.

Pizarro's men were eager to return to civilization. They staggered toward the messenger's boat, their feet and skin bleeding from sores, their heads dizzy from sunstroke. Some of them yelled at Pizarro. He was nothing more than a butcher, they charged, willing to risk the lives of his men on a doomed treasure hunt.

Pizarro unsheathed his sword and drew a line in the sandy beach. "Gentlemen," he said, pointing south of the line toward Peru, "on that side are toil, hunger, nakedness, the drenching storm, desertion, and death."

Then he pointed to the other side of the line: "On this side, ease and pleasure. But over there, God willing, lie the great riches of the earth. Choose, each man, what best becomes a brave [Spaniard]."

Pizarro stepped over the line. "For my part," he said, "I go south."

CHAPTER 8

Homecoming

PIZARRO FINDS GOLD
and returns to his
hometown.

THIRTEEN MEN FOLLOWED PIZARRO OVER his line in the sand. The others returned to Panama.

In 1527, Almagro returned to Pizarro's island refuge with a relief ship. He had convinced Pedro de los Ríos, the new governor of Panama, that Pizarro was close to finding a golden city. Governor Ríos agreed to extend the expedition for six months.

With Almagro, Pizarro sailed farther south. Docking at the Bay of Tumbes, he saw more Indian villages—

rows of mud and stone houses, balsa rafts along the shore, and fields of crops.

At the village of Tumbes, the local Tumpis Indians welcomed the Spaniards into their homes. They fed the invaders sweet potatoes and maize—foods the Europeans had never seen. For the first time, the Spaniards saw llamas, which they called "Peruvian sheep." The Tumpis were fascinated by the Spaniards' dark beards. They were fearful of the Spanish guns— "thunder sticks," as the Indians called them. According to the Spaniards, the Indians believed that spirits exploded from their barrels when angered.

At Tumbes, Pizarro finally saw what he hungered for—gold. The village leaders wore so much gold in their ears that their lobes were extended and deformed. Pizarro toured an Indian temple decorated in gold. The Tumpis echoed the now-familiar words to Pizarro: A much greater golden empire lay farther south.

Pizzaro and his crew continued a bit farther south. But by this time, they were too

DESCENDANTS OF THE INCA still live in Peru. This modern-day woman leads her llama past a stone wall made by the Inca.

tired to continue. They returned to Panama, hoping to convince Governor Ríos to approve a larger expedition. According to one of Pizarro's men, they brought with them "llamas, gold and silver, and woolen garments of many colors." Pizarro had also persuaded the Tumpis to give him two boys to work as translators.

But Governor Ríos refused to allow a third expedition. He had tired of the explorer's recklessness. Pizarro had far exceeded his six-month time limit. He had lost dozens of men to starvation, disease, and Indian arrows— and for what? A few trinkets of gold, silver, and wool?

Pizarro didn't give up. In 1528, he returned to Spain and appeared before Charles V, the current king of Spain. Pizarro begged the king to support another mission. Charles agreed and named Pizarro governor of all the lands he might discover. He ordered Pizarro to find 250 men to join his mission.

The conquistador returned to his hometown of Trujillo to look for volunteers. Even in rugged Extremadura, he had trouble recruiting soldiers. It was known, no doubt, that no one had gotten rich from Pizarro's expeditions. Dozens, however, had died or come back broken in body and spirit.

But Pizarro did convince 17 men from Trujillo to join him, including his much younger half brothers—Hernando, Juan, and Gonzalo. Finally, by January 1530, Pizarro had scraped together 120 men and left Seville for Panama.

In December, with three ships, 180 men, and 27 horses, Pizarro and Almagro sailed south from Panama, headed for Peru. As one of Pizarro's soldiers put it, "When in ancient or modern times has so great an enterprise been undertaken by so few against so many odds . . . to conquer the unknown?"

PART 2

The Conquest of

Peru

CHAPTER 9

Into the Empire

Pizarro and his crew approach the
GREAT INCA CIVILIZATION.

PIZARRO'S SHIPS ARRIVED ON THE
outskirts of the Inca Empire in March 1531. He
had intended to return to Tumbes, the gold-rich
coast where the Tumpis had welcomed the Spaniards
ashore. But fierce storms forced him to land
farther north.

Eventually, the Spaniards reached a smaller
Indian village where they were invited to rest. The
conquistadors noticed that, even in this small settlement,
the people wore gold and silver ornaments.

Pizarro and his crew had no idea what lay just to the south. They were about to encounter perhaps the mightiest Indian civilization of all time—the Inca Empire. The Inca presided over a vast and sophisticated culture, dwarfing even that of the mighty Aztecs to the north. By the time Pizarro arrived, the Inca Empire stretched 2,500 miles from north to south. It was so enormous that Indians referred to it as "the four quarters of the world."

The Inca built their power and wealth by conquering smaller Indian nations. From 1200 to 1400, Inca armies defeated dozens of smaller tribes. Inca emperors brought the tribes into the empire, forcing them to turn over taxes to the central government and soldiers to the Inca army.

At the center of the empire stood several large cities. Stone houses fanned out around sprawling central squares. Huge temples were built into mountainsides. The buildings were marvels of early architecture. The Inca had no cement, so blocks of stones were carved to fit perfectly together. And since the Inca hadn't discovered the wheel, they relied on sheer muscle to move their building materials.

Inca emperors linked the remote corners of their empire with a vast network of roads. The roads were built for pack llamas and foot traffic and snaked for miles between small villages. In the mountains, road builders made the world's first suspension bridges out of vines and reeds.

The Inca's military conquests made the empire unimaginably rich. The Inca took control of the gold and silver mines of the region, which produced enormous treasures. The most important members of Inca society wore clothing strung with gold thread. They ate from gold plates and cups. Their religious temples were richer than anything the Spaniards had ever seen.

The Inca worshipped Inti, the sun god, and the Inca emperor was considered to be Inti in human form. Inti could be kind, blessing the people with good harvests

THE INCA BUILT MAGNIFICENT CITIES—and the
conquistadors did their best to destroy them. But one city, Machu Picchu,
remained hidden from the Spaniards. Sometimes called "the lost city of the
Inca," Machu Picchu was unknown to most of the world until 1911.
Today, people can visit the ruins of this ancient city.

and health. But he was quick to anger. The Inca routinely practiced human sacrifices to keep Inti's anger at bay. Women, children, and slaves were regularly carried to mountaintops and killed to appease him.

For nearly a year, Pizarro and his men could only imagine the extent of the vast Inca Empire. They were stuck on its northern edge, slowed by disease, hunger, and bad weather.

Finally, in December 1531, an Extremaduran named Hernando de Soto arrived with 100 fresh soldiers. The 31-year-old de Soto must have given the Spaniards new hope. He was respected for his bravery and his skill as a horseman. Pizarro made de Soto a captain, and the men settled in to wait out the winter rains.

THE INCA ICE MAIDEN

IN 1995, ARCHEOLOGIST JOHAN REINHARD was climbing Mount Ampato, a 20,000-foot peak in the Andes, when he saw a large bundle on the ground. From a distance, the explorer thought it was a backpack. Then his heart began to race.

Reinhard had found the 500-year-old body of a young Inca girl. He named her Juanita. And she has helped historians get a glimpse of a lost civilization.

Juanita was almost certainly a human sacrifice. One day in the late 1400s, she was dressed in bright robes and led up Mount Ampato. Some gold trinkets found near her were probably offered as a gift to the sun god.

X-rays showed that Juanita's skull had been crushed. Most likely, an Inca priest had bludgeoned her to death. It sounds horrible, but Inca families often offered their teenage daughters to the gods. They believed that the sacrifices kept their people safe from droughts and earthquakes.

JUANITA, an Inca sacrifice.

Signs of War

Pizarro finds an empire
TORN APART BY CIVIL WAR.

THE WINTER STORMS ENDED IN THE spring of 1532, and Pizarro's ships were finally able to sail to Tumbes. But the scene at the bay shocked even the battle-worn conquistadors. The village where they had once found shelter now lay in ruins. Homes were destroyed. Crops were burnt. The ground was littered with corpses covered in flies and maggots.

From the few survivors, Pizarro learned that the great Inca Empire was being torn apart by a civil war between two half brothers.

From 1493 to 1525, the Inca had been ruled by the aging emperor Huayna Capac. In the last years of his reign, smallpox—brought by the Europeans—had struck the Inca. In 1525, Huayna Capac himself caught the disease. Within a few days, he was dead.

The emperor's death set off a fierce civil war between two of his sons, the half brothers Atahualpa and Huascar. Over the course of a year, more than 100,000 Inca were killed by their two armies.

In May 1532, as Pizarro was leaving Tumbes, Atahualpa's generals cornered Huascar's army near the Inca capital of Cuzco. Atahualpa had Huascar captured and locked in a wooden cage. Atahualpa's men forced Huascar to watch as his wives and children were slaughtered. The victims' bodies were impaled on stakes and displayed on the road into Cuzco for Huascar's followers to see. Within a year, Huascar would be executed as well.

Pizarro saw signs of this civil war as he and his crew marched deeper inland. Dead bodies were strewn

THE FEARSOME WARRIOR ATAHUALPA battled his brother
Huascar for control of the Inca Empire.

about the trails. Abandoned villages and farmland had been burned.

For two months, the conquistadors slogged their way through the jungle, looking for the grand Inca cities that supposedly lay to the south.

In June, they arrived in the village of Tangarara, where they heard more stories of Atahualpa's power and ruthlessness. Sweating in their armor, many of Pizarro's men must have wondered whether they had signed on to a suicide mission.

Pizarro told his troops that any who feared the unknown could stay in Tangarara and wait for a ship back to Spain. "With the rest," he proclaimed, "be they many or few, I shall pursue this adventure to the end."

Only seven men stayed behind. The rest continued into the heart of the Inca Empire.

CHAPTER 11

Over the Mountains

The tiny band of Spaniards finally FINDS THE GREAT INCA ARMY.

As PIZARRO MARCHED SOUTHWARD, HE probably knew he was being watched. Atahualpa's scouts kept a close eye on the Spaniards. The emperor and his army were camped in the Cajamarca valley, 300 miles south of Tumbes. From there, Atahualpa followed Pizarro's progress and debated with his generals about the best course of action. They decided not to attack the Spaniards. After all, there were thousands of soldiers in the south still loyal to Huascar. They seemed to pose a much greater threat to Atahualpa than 180 sick and starving Spaniards.

Pizarro pressed farther south, assuming that each step brought him closer to the Inca emperor. Along the way, he pressured Indian tribes to ally with him. Those who were hostile to Atahualpa often agreed to help. Indians who resisted were treated brutally. Outside of Tumbes, Pizarro had 13 Indians executed for refusing to help him.

Pizarro's captain, Hernando de Soto, acted with a similar ruthlessness. In September 1532, he entered a city called Cajas and demanded that its cacique turn over 500 women to be enslaved by the Spaniards.

Also at Cajas, de Soto learned exactly where Atahualpa was camped. Pizarro sent an Inca lord ahead with gifts for the emperor. Then he led his men into the Andes Mountains toward Atahualpa's camp at Cajamarca.

The tired Spanish soldiers climbed the snow-covered peaks. They led their mules and horses along

PIZARRO LEADS HIS MEN through the Andes. During the
journey, many men and pack animals fell to their deaths.

narrow stone trails chiseled into the mountainside. The Spaniards climbed as high as 13,000 feet. As they inched forward, soldiers crept along the paths. Some slipped and fell screaming thousands of feet to the rocks below. Giant condors swooped past, sending startled men tumbling to their deaths.

Finally, after several days in the mountains, Pizarro's party spied the valley of Cajamarca. Nursing frostbitten hands and feet, the Spaniards looked down on a huge city of houses made of stone and brick. Beyond it lay a fearsome sight: the Inca army's campsite—two miles of tents with tens of thousands of warriors.

For the first time, Pizarro may have realized that the odds were stacked against him. His men certainly wondered how they could defeat such a mighty army. "The spectacle caused . . . fear in the stoutest heart," said one soldier. "But it was too late to turn back."

CHAPTER 12

The Battle of Cajamarca

PIZARRO LAYS A TRAP
for the sun god.

ON NOVEMBER 15, 1532, PIZARRO AND HIS men descended into the valley in a hailstorm and took refuge in the city of Cajamarca. According to one Spaniard, it was bigger than any city in Spain. Pizarro's secretary, Francisco de Xeres, said that Cajamarca was "surrounded by strong walls, three times the height of a man, much better built than any we had seen before." A giant temple to the sun god towered over one corner of the city.

Shortly after the Spaniards arrived, a messenger from Atahualpa came to assure Pizarro that the emperor meant no harm to the Spaniards. Pizarro, who had seen the results of Atahualpa's wrath in village after village, was skeptical.

De Soto pressed Pizarro to let him visit Atahualpa in his vast camp outside the city walls of Cajamarca. Pizarro agreed, sending de Soto with five or six horsemen and a priest named Friar Vicente Valverde.

The tiny party rode to the great Inca camp and made their way proudly through rows of warriors armed with lances and bows. Atahualpa was seated outside a bathhouse with several of his wives. "Hernando de Soto rode right up to him," Friar Vicente reported, "and so close to him was he that his horse's nose touched his headdress."

The Inca warriors had never seen a horse before, and several of them drew back in fear. But Atahualpa stood firm. He accepted the gift of a ring from de Soto and then disappeared into his bathhouse. Later, Friar

Vicente reported, the emperor executed more than 300 of his men for showing their fear of the horsemen.

Several days later, Pizarro's brother Hernando met with Atahualpa in the emperor's camp. Over goblets of maize wine, Hernando told Atahualpa that the Spaniards had come in peace. They simply wanted to teach the Inca the Christian faith. Hernando invited Atahualpa to visit Pizarro in the city of Cajamarca, and Atahualpa agreed. Little did the emperor know he would be walking into a trap.

The next day, Pizarro's secretary, Xeres, watched from the city gates as Atahualpa approached with a large bodyguard. "It was as if the entire valley was in movement," Xeres wrote. Atahualpa "was carried in a throne chair on the shoulders of his lords. Six hundred Indians in white and black livery as if pieces of a chessboard came ahead of him, sweeping the roads of stones and branches . . . wearing headdresses of gold and silver." To the surprise of the Spaniards, the Inca were mostly unarmed.

ATAHUALPA IS CARRIED to his meeting with Pizarro
on a throne. Convinced that he could not be harmed, Atahualpa
did not bring his best warriors with him. It was a fatal mistake.

Atahualpa's men crowded into Cajamarca's central square, singing war songs about the emperor's strength. There was no one there to greet them. "What has become of the bearded ones?" Atahualpa asked one of his generals.

Just then, Friar Vicente appeared. Through a translator, he explained that Pizarro was an ambassador from a great king overseas. The king wanted to be

Atahualpa's friend, he said, but only if the emperor accepted the will of God and converted to Christianity.

Atahualpa asked how the priest knew the will of gods. Friar Vicente held up a book of prayer and said that it contained the words of God.

Having no written language, Atahualpa had probably never seen a book. He demanded that the priest give him the book. After looking at it for a minute, he threw it to the ground. Insulted by the priest's demands, he turned to his bodyguards and commanded, "Let none of them escape!"

Suddenly, the Spaniards came out of hiding and swarmed into the square. Pizarro and 24 soldiers surged forward with their shields and swords. More Spanish soldiers streamed over walls and jumped from rooftops. Sixty horsemen thundered into the square. Atahualpa's guards were attacked with swords and lances, harquebuses and crossbows. There were fewer than 200 Spaniards, yet to the Inca, they must have seemed like a fearsome army.

Xeres described the battle: "The guns were fired off, the trumpets sounded and the troops, both horse and foot, sallied forth. On seeing the horses charge, many of the Indians . . . fled. The horsemen rode them down, killing and wounding and following in pursuit."

Pizarro and his soldiers pushed through the crowd surrounding Atahualpa. Pizarro himself pulled the emperor from his gold throne. He ordered his men not to harm Atahualpa. "Let no one who values his life strike him," Pizarro shouted.

For about half an hour, Pizarro's men slaughtered the confused Inca. Thousands of Indians lay dead in the valley by the time it was over. Thousands more had fled when their sun god was captured. The most powerful ruler in South America had been defeated. And not a single Spanish soldier had been killed.

ARMED AND DANGEROUS

HOW DID FEWER THAN 200 SPANIARDS DEFEAT thousands of Inca bodyguards—in less than an hour?

The Spanish had the best equipment from Europe. They wore steel breastplates and chain mail. The Inca had wooden helmets and reinforced cotton for armor.

The Spanish used harquebuses, crossbows, and swords and daggers made of steel. Most of the Inca fought with slingshots, bows and arrows, and wooden lances.

The Spanish also had horses, which they used like tanks, barreling through Indian defenses.

What's more, Atahualpa left his best warriors in camp, assuming that his presence would be enough to intimidate the Spaniards. When he was captured, his warriors had no will to fight. They fled, and an entire empire began to fall apart.

ATAHUALPA'S THRONE
surrounded by Pizarro's men.

CHAPTER 13

The Ransom

THE EMPEROR GATHERS THE TREASURES of a civilization for his captors.

ATAHUALPA, THE MIGHTY EMPEROR AND a god to his people, was now a prisoner. His warriors, seeing their leader humiliated, deserted Cajamarca.

On his first night as a captive, Atahualpa dined with Pizarro, not as a prisoner but as an equal. They ate in a large banquet hall overlooking the Cajamarca square where the bodies of 2,000 slain Inca warriors still lay.

Each night, guards chained Atahualpa into a stone house converted into a prison. Pizarro allowed

Atahualpa's wives and servants to stay with the emperor. Atahualpa continued to eat from gold plates. And the conquistadors were ordered to treat him with respect.

Word of Atahualpa's defeat spread quickly to nearby tribes. One by one, caciques who had owed their loyalty to the emperor came to pledge their allegiance to Pizarro.

For Pizarro, however, the war was far from over. At least 100,000 soldiers were still loyal to Atahualpa. Many of them were camped within a week's march of Cajamarca.

During an early meeting in his cell, Atahualpa offered three rooms full of gold and silver to Pizarro as ransom for his life. As his messengers went out to collect the treasure, Atahualpa tried to befriend his captors. De Soto taught the emperor to play chess and dice. Hernando, the only Pizarro who could read and write, taught Atahualpa to speak basic Spanish.

Both de Soto and Hernando had very narrow attitudes about the Indians and were amazed by Atahualpa's intelligence. As Xeres explains, they were

INCA EMPEROR ATAHUALPA raises his hand to show how much gold he will give the Spaniards in exchange for his freedom.

"astounded to find so much wisdom in a barbarian."

As time passed, Pizarro grew tired of waiting for the ransom. In January 1533, he sent his brother Hernando out to gather loot.

In May, Pizarro's old partner Almagro arrived in Cajamarca with about 200 fresh soldiers. He was just in time to see Hernando return from his looting trip in the south. Hernando had brought with him a vast load of treasure to add to Atahualpa's ransom. One observer said, "There were jars and vats, great and small pitchers, pots, braziers, shields, and many other objects made of gold and silver."

THE INCA COLLECT GOLD items for Atahualpa's ransom.

When the ransom was complete, Pizarro ordered nine forges to be built. For months, day and night, Inca goldsmiths fed the treasures of their empire into the fires. Statues and shields; bowls, plates, and goblets; rings and necklaces—all were melted down and molded into bars.

Hernando left in June to carry one-fifth of the loot back to Spain. The rest was divided among the captains and their men.

CHAPTER 14

Betrayal!

With the ransom paid, THE INCA EMPEROR'S LIFE GROWS CHEAP.

ATAHUALPA'S RANSOM HAD BEEN PAID. But that didn't mean that Pizarro was planning to keep his end of the deal and free the emperor. As soon as the gold and silver had been collected, Almagro began to insist that Atahualpa be executed. Kill the emperor, Almagro said, and he wouldn't be able to rally his troops against the Spaniards.

Pizarro was unsure. The Spanish king, Charles V, had not approved such an action. And what if the Inca decided to avenge the death of Atahualpa?

Finally, Pizarro made a decision. On the evening of July 26, 1533, Atahualpa was shackled and led to the torch-lit city square. Guards tied his neck to a stake. He cried out to his captors, "Why are you going to kill me? What have I or my sons or my wives ever done to you?" Atahualpa lowered his hands to his knees to show the height of his young children. He pleaded with Pizarro to spare him for his children's sake. The emperor's servants and wives watched from inside his cell, wailing and banging on the stone walls.

Pizarro was unmoved. But he offered the emperor the conquistadors' version of mercy. Since Atahualpa wasn't a Christian, Spanish law demanded that he be burned to death. Pizarro promised him a quick death by strangulation if he converted to Christianity. Atahualpa, who may have thought he was being offered his freedom, agreed.

"[Atahualpa] wept and spoke to the interpreter," one soldier noted, "and again he asked [Pizarro] to care for his . . . sons and daughters."

Pizarro gave a signal. The rope around Atahualpa's neck was quickly wrenched. His head snapped to one side, and he was dead. The lifeless body of the Inca's last great emperor was left in the city square, while his wives and servants wept through the night.

EVEN AFTER Atahualpa's ransom had been paid, Pizarro had him put to death.

Francisco Pizarro in Pictures

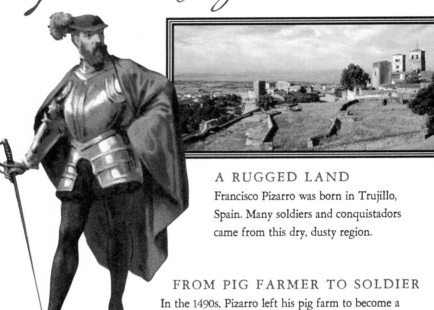

A RUGGED LAND

Francisco Pizarro was born in Trujillo, Spain. Many soldiers and conquistadors came from this dry, dusty region.

FROM PIG FARMER TO SOLDIER

In the 1490s, Pizarro left his pig farm to become a soldier in the fearsome Spanish army.

A GRUELING TRIP

Hearing tales of gold and riches in the New World, Pizarro joined an expedition to Hispaniola. The voyage across the Atlantic Ocean was long, dangerous, and tedious.

Vasco Nuñez toma posesion de la Mar del Sur

THE "OTHER SEA"

In 1513, Pizarro and other soldiers accompanied Vasco de Balboa on his expedition to find what would become known as the Pacific Ocean.

TRUST ME

Pizarro formed a partnership with Diego de Almagro to explore Peru. A priest provided some of the cash. They all shook hands and agreed to split the profits.

"FOR MY PART, I GO SOUTH"

Stranded on the western coast of South America, Pizarro's starving men wanted to abandon their quest for Peru. Pizarro drew a line in the sand and challenged them to stick with him.

AN EMPIRE OF GOLD

Conquistadors like Pizarro spent much of their lives looking for gold. And the Inca Empire had a lot of it. To the left is an Inca earring.

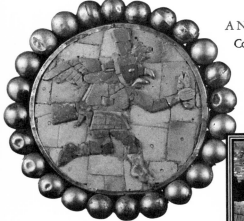

STRONG DEFENSE

The Inca relied on sheer human strength to build fortresses out of huge stones.

A NETWORK OF ROADS

Inca emperors linked the corners of their empire with roads built for pack llamas and foot traffic. The roads snaked for miles between small villages.

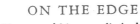

ON THE EDGE
Pizarro and his men climbed dangerous passes in the Andes to reach Emperor Atahualpa.

THE LAST EMPEROR

Pizarro assured Atahualpa that he had come in peace. But when the Inca emperor arrived for a meeting with Pizarro, the Spaniards ambushed him.

RANSOM OF GOLD

After he was captured, Atahualpa showed Pizarro how much treasure he would give the Spaniards in exchange for his freedom. He promised he could fill the room with gold and twice more with silver.

THE INCA ENSLAVED

After burning and looting the Inca capital of Cuzco in 1533, Pizarro's men enslaved the local people.

A RIVAL'S END

Over the years, Pizarro and his partner Almagro had many disagreements. In their final conflict, Pizarro had Almagro put to death.

A CONQUERED CONQUISTADOR

In 1977, Pizarro's skull was found in Lima, Peru. He had been killed in 1541 by Almagro's son, Diego.

PART 3

Ruling an Empire

CHAPTER 15

Cuzco in Flames

Pizarro captures the Inca capital and
REMAKES THE EMPIRE.

THE INCA EMPEROR WAS DEAD. CONTROL
of his kingdom—and its riches—now lay within
Pizarro's grasp.

But conquering the Inca wasn't going to be easy.
The capital city of Cuzco still lay under Inca control.
It was defended by one of Atahualpa's former chiefs,
Quisquis, and at least 10,000 warriors. Pizarro had just a
few hundred men.

Pizarro's plan was to select a new Inca emperor
who would rule as a puppet while Pizarro gave the

orders. He chose one of Huascar's younger brothers, Tupac Huallpa. At a public ceremony, Inca priests crowned the young boy emperor. The new "emperor" then knelt before Pizarro and swore loyalty to the conquistador and to King Charles V of Spain.

Sixteen days after Atahualpa's execution, Pizarro's army marched out of Cajamarca, headed for Cuzco. The party was enormous—a long line of Spanish soldiers, tribal warriors, mules, and llamas. It took nearly a full day to leave the city.

The party trekked along stone roads and narrow mountain passes. Along the way, Tupac Huallpa died of smallpox. Pizarro quickly replaced him with another of Huascar's brothers, a 16-year-old named Manco.

Climbing high into the Andes, Pizarro's army finally reached Cuzco in November 1533. From the mountains, Pizarro's men looked down at the city in the valley below.

The Inca capital was magnificent. Stone palaces circled its gigantic central square. A stone fortress large enough to hold 5,000 soldiers overlooked the city from the mountainside. An enormous temple dominated the center of the city. It held the mummies of dead emperors and a huge sculpture of the sun made of solid gold. As Pizarro's aide wrote, Cuzco was "grand and beautiful. . . . No poor people live there, and each lord possesses a palace . . . painted and constructed in stone."

Wary of the approaching army, Chief Quisquis and his army had evacuated the capital. With the Inca warriors gone, Pizarro was able to make a grand entrance into Cuzco. He marched three columns of soldiers through the city square. Thousands of the city's residents lined the streets to watch.

In the middle of Cuzco, Pizarro proclaimed Manco the new emperor. He placed a wreath on the teen's head. Then Manco gave a speech, pledging his loyalty to the Spanish king and to Pizarro himself.

The Inca of Cuzco, many of whom had supported Huascar in the civil war, celebrated Manco's coronation.

THE INCA CAPITAL OF CUZCO, located high in the Andes Mountains, dazzled the Spaniards. The city was home to about 200,000 Inca.

PIZARRO'S ARMY MARCHED into the city of Cuzco in 1533.
He supposedly ordered his men not to loot the magnificent capital,
but they could not be controlled.

But the celebration was short-lived. Within hours of Pizarro's march into Cuzco, the conquistador's tired, desperate troops ransacked the city. Drunk on the local maize wine, the soldiers set fires throughout the Inca capital. They looted Cuzco's palaces and temples. They hacked down gold walls and destroyed homes. They tortured Indians to find more gold. They even dug up the dead to steal jewelry from the corpses.

Manco quietly watched the Spaniards terrorize his people. He didn't raise a hand to stop the conquistadors. But he despaired over the fate of his people. An Indian witness later testified that Manco cursed the Spaniards. "These are not the sons of God," he swore, "but the sons of the Devil."

SWEAT OF THE SUN

THE INCA EMPIRE WAS BUILT ON GOLD. Temple walls were plated with gold sheets. The emperor sat on a golden throne. Priests wore robes woven with fine golden thread. Life-size gold statues of everything from past emperors to llamas decorated the great cities.

To the Inca, gold had sacred value. They believed that it came from the gods. It was, as they put it, "the sweat of the sun." To the Spaniards, gold was nothing but money. Pizarro melted down most of the great works of Inca art into bars that were easy to transport.

The Spaniards' hunger for gold amused at least one Inca artist. Centuries after Pizarro, archeologists found an Inca cartoon depicting an Indian talking to a Spaniard. The Indian asks, "Do you actually eat this gold?" The Spaniard replies, "Yes, we do!"

INCA TREASURES: a woman, an alpaca, and a llama.

CHAPTER 16

"Take Away Their Gold"

PIZARRO EXPANDS HIS POWER in Peru.

FROM HIS POST IN CUZCO, PIZARRO shrewdly and ruthlessly extended his control over the Inca Empire. First, he prepared to defend Cuzco, placing many of his men in its fortress and keeping a squadron of horsemen on alert at all times. Then he distributed the city's gold among his soldiers. He awarded his officers palaces and women. As one Spanish soldier wrote: "All the land, houses, and [llamas] of this city and valley were divided and given to those who conquered this city and kingdom."

What the soldier did not mention is that Pizarro also gave away the Inca people. He divided the land surrounding the city into 88 districts called *encomiendas*. The Spanish rulers of each district—

THE SPANISH CONQUISTADORS DIVIDED the lands and treasures of the Inca Empire among themselves. They forced many of the Inca to work as their slaves.

known as *encomenderos*—were given the right to tax the Indians who lived there and use them as laborers or soldiers. Under the law of their conquerors, the Inca had become virtual slaves.

Some of the richest land grants went to men of the church. King Charles V had made converting the Indians a high priority. Shortly after Pizarro's victory, Catholic missionaries began arriving in Peru. Some priests tried to protect the Indians from the worst of the Spaniards. Friar Vicente, for one, urged Pizarro to treat them well and encourage their conversion to Christianity. Pizarro reportedly answered, "I did not come here for [religious] reasons. I came here to take away their gold."

Still, mindful of his duty to his king, Pizarro named Friar Vicente the first bishop of Cuzco. He ordered the destruction of the city's sun temples and erected a Catholic church in Cuzco's main square.

Pizarro spent the first eight months of 1534 battling the last of Atahualpa's forces. He sent de Soto and

Almagro north with bands of Spanish and Indian soldiers. By August, they had defeated the armies still loyal to Atahualpa.

Pizarro then set out to explore the Peruvian coast in search of a new capital for Peru. Cuzco, sitting high in the mountains, had no access to water. Without a port, goods and travelers could not easily be transported. In 1535, Pizarro located a much more suitable location for a capital. Near a peaceful harbor on the Pacific coast, he founded the city that would later be named Lima.

But before he could build his new city, the conquistador got word that the Spaniards in Cuzco were engaged in a bitter dispute. Almagro was fighting Pizarro's brothers for control of Cuzco. De Soto was caught in the middle, trying to keep the two parties from falling into open warfare.

Pizarro returned to Cuzco and managed to trick Almagro into giving up his claim to Cuzco. He convinced Almagro to pursue even greater riches to the south, in present-day Chile.

For a time, the peace held in Cuzco. Pizarro returned to Lima. Hernando de Soto set off for Spain by way of Panama with a caravan of llamas carrying his vast Inca fortune. Now famous, de Soto would later set out for Florida in search of more riches. He never found another fortune in gold, but he was likely the first white man to cross the Mississippi River. De Soto died on the river's banks in 1542, the victim of an arrow wound.

CHAPTER 17

Siege!

The Inca launch a last effort to RECLAIM THEIR EMPIRE.

WITH ALMAGRO AND DE SOTO GONE, the Pizarro brothers took charge in Cuzco. Relations between the Spanish and the Inca deteriorated quickly.

The Pizarros horrified the Inca with their treatment of Manco, the young man chosen as emperor. First, the Spaniards forced Manco to turn over his wife as a slave. Soon after, Manco tried to flee the city. The Spaniards caught him and dragged him back, his neck tied to the tail of Gonzalo Pizarro's horse.

The Spaniards then tortured the emperor. According to one Indian account: "Juan and Gonzalo Pizarro mistreated [Manco] . . . placing him in irons and imprisoning him. . . . His guards urinated and spat in his face, calling him a dog and threatening to burn him alive. . . . His treatment was so cruel that . . . he cried out that if they did not strangle him he would strangle himself."

The Inca were outraged. Some quietly planned a rebellion, while others led raids on Spanish outposts. In a village near Cuzco, the bodies of two conquistadors were found with their throats slit. According to one report, Juan and Gonzalo took their revenge by trapping 8,000 Indians in a mountain fort and massacring them all.

Eventually, Manco managed to escape and assemble an army. Word spread throughout the land that the young emperor was free and would lead a rebellion against the Spaniards.

In February 1536, an army of 100,000 Inca surrounded the capital. The Pizarro brothers took cover in the fortress overlooking the city.

THE INCA EMPEROR MANCO had finally had enough. He raised an army of 100,000 Inca to fight the Spanish in 1536.

Manco's archers shot burning arrows over the walls. Juan Pizarro was struck on the head by a rock hurled from an Inca slingshot. He died days later.

The Inca laid siege to Cuzco for nearly six months. They blocked the mountain passes from Lima to prevent Francisco Pizarro from sending help. Trapped in the fortress, the Spaniards, led by Hernando Pizarro, seemed doomed. But eventually, Hernando and his men were rescued by an old acquaintance.

In August 1536, Diego de Almagro returned from Chile. His men had suffered through a harrowing journey in the Andes. He had lost dozens of soldiers to cold, hunger, and Indian attacks. Perhaps worst of all, he had failed to find treasure. Now, he was determined to return to Peru and claim Cuzco.

Almagro's men arrived at the outskirts of Cuzco and joined the fight against the Inca. As Hernando battled Manco's army from inside the city, Almagro attacked them from behind.

Emperor Manco was forced into retreat, and Almagro marched into Cuzco. The one-eyed conquistador immediately seized Hernando Pizarro. According to Friar Vicente, Hernando was "continually kept in heavy chains" inside a small stone cell.

Almagro had tired of Francisco Pizarro and his brothers. He vowed to finally rid himself of them once and for all.

CHAPTER 18

The Almagro War

Pizarro battles his old partner for CONTROL OF THE EMPIRE.

ALMAGRO'S GENERAL, RODRIGO DE Orgonez, urged Almagro to kill Hernando and Gonzalo before their brother Francisco arrived from Lima. If left alive, the Pizarros would surely seek revenge. As General Orgonez said, "A Pizarro was never known to forget an injury."

Almagro decided to spare the Pizarros' lives. By then, Francisco Pizarro had learned of his brothers' plight. He arranged a meeting with Almagro just outside of Lima to bargain for their release.

Pizarro and Almagro met on November 13, 1537. The two conquistadors were both in their late sixties. They had fought together for many years. Still, they hated and mistrusted each other.

Almagro rode toward Pizarro. He dismounted and extended his arms to embrace his old partner. But Pizarro snubbed his greeting, merely touching the tip of his helmet. "By what authority," Pizarro demanded, "have you taken possession of Cuzco, which I won after so much hardship? And what gave you the right . . . to imprison my brothers?"

Almagro was indignant. Cuzco belonged to him, he insisted. He would determine the Pizarro brothers' fate.

Pizarro appeared to back down. He offered to let Almagro keep the Inca capital without a fight if he set the brothers free.

After consulting with his aides, Almagro agreed— even though General Orgonez once again warned him not to trust Pizarro. Orgonez was right. Pizarro had no intention of handing Cuzco over to Almagro. As soon as Hernando and Gonzalo were released, the Pizarros made plans to reclaim the city. In April 1538, Hernando led an army across the mountains toward Cuzco to face Almagro's troops.

On April 26, 1538, the two armies met near Cuzco. General Orgonez led Almagro's army—500 conquistadors backed by 10,000 Inca warriors who hated the Pizarros. His soldiers lined the banks of the Las Salinas River. Across the water, Hernando Pizarro, in full armor with an orange cape, commanded an army of 700 men.

General Orgonez spurred his horse. He yelled to his troops: "Follow me who will! I ride to my death!" He galloped into the river as Hernando's army raced forward.

Amid cannon blasts and gunfire, the two armies fought waist-deep in the river. A harquebus shot hit General Orgonez in the forehead, splitting open his armored helmet. Bleeding from his head, the general killed two more men with a lance. As his troops

ALMAGRO AND PIZARRO had done their best to swindle each other.
The competition ended in 1538, when Pizarro had his partner put to death.

retreated, General Orgonez yelled to them, "By Our Lord, I thought we had come here to fight." The words were barely out of his mouth when one of Pizarro's horseman raced behind Orgonez and, with a slash of his sword, cut off Orgonez's head.

Pizarro's soldiers eventually forced Almagro's men to retreat. When the Inca saw what was happening, they deserted and looted the bodies of the dead Spaniards. Hernando Pizarro captured Almagro. He dragged Almagro back to Cuzco and locked him in the same small stone cell where Hernando himself had been kept prisoner.

Almagro spent three months in the cell. The once proud conquistador was sickly, broken, and tearful. On July 8, 1538, Almagro was chained to a stake and strangled. Then his head was cut off and stuck on the end of a lance, his one eye still open. Hernando paraded Almagro's head among the Spaniards and Inca.

That was the price for crossing the Pizarro brothers.

CHAPTER 19

Die by the Sword

The mighty conquistador
MEETS HIS END.

Francisco Pizarro now reigned as
the unquestioned leader of Peru. In 1539, he returned
to Cuzco triumphant. He marched into the city in full
battle armor, wearing an ornate gilded breastplate.
Trumpets heralded his arrival.

Pizarro awarded the men who fought for him with
gold—and all of Almagro's lands and possessions.
Almagro's wealth was supposed to be inherited by
his 18-year-old son, also named Diego. But Pizarro
claimed it for himself. And he had Diego confined to a

house in Lima, near Pizarro's own palace. His message was clear: Your life is in my hands.

Pizarro was obliged to send a fifth of his fortune back to Spain. Once again, he chose his brother Hernando to take the gold to King Charles. Before leaving, Hernando warned Pizarro to keep a close eye on young Diego and his men. "If you let them assemble," Hernando said, "they will kill you . . . and nothing will be left of your memory."

Hernando departed with packs of llamas and enslaved Inca to carry his vast fortune. The two brothers would never see each other again. After making the long sea voyage to Spain, Hernando was immediately arrested for the murder of Almagro.

By this time, King Charles was wary of the conquistadors in Peru. The stories of warring packs of Spaniards concerned him. Charles worried that Pizarro had become too powerful. He sent officials to Peru to control the old conquistador.

Diego saw Pizarro's position weakening. The

OUTRAGED THAT PIZARRO had taken his father's life—and his own
inheritance—Diego Almagro hired assassins to kill the aged conquistador.

vengeful teenager wanted to act fast. Pizarro heard rumors that Diego would try to assassinate him. But, like Atahualpa, Pizarro underestimated the threat.

On June 26, 1541, 20 of Diego's heavily armed supporters stormed Pizarro's palace in Lima. Pizarro was dining with his friends. He jumped to his feet. "Traitors!" he yelled. "Have you come to kill me in my own home!"

Pizarro struggled to put on his armor as his bodyguards were killed. Nearly 70 years old, Pizarro attacked his assassins with his sword. He killed two of them and ran through a third. As he tried to free his sword, an assassin's knife sliced his throat. Pizarro fell to the floor, where his attackers stabbed him again and again.

As Pizarro lay on the ground gasping for breath, the conquistador supposedly drew a cross in a pool of his own blood. Seconds later, he was dead.

Wicked?

In June 1977, a team of construction workers were restoring the basement of a cathedral in Lima. They came across a metal box sealed within the church walls. When they opened it, they discovered a man's skull and bones, along with a sword and silver spurs. The box had an inscription on it that read: "This is the head of . . . Francisco Pizarro who discovered and conquered these realms of Peru."

Pizarro's remains had lain hidden in that church for more than 400 years after his murder by the supporters of Diego Almagro.

Pizarro's grave may be inconspicuous, but his legacy is not. During his 11 years in Peru, he dismantled an empire and a culture that had thrived for nearly four centuries. He introduced the Spanish language and the Catholic religion to Peru. Both still dominate today. He established the city of Lima, which became a center of commerce and art on the continent.

LLAMAS CARRY TREASURE stolen from the Inca by the Spanish.

To the Inca of Peru, Pizarro was a ruthless vandal. After the conquest, the Inca were reduced to near slavery in their own country. They had to pay high taxes to the district lords appointed by Pizarro. They harvested potatoes and corn in blistering heat. Others toiled at backbreaking labor in gold and silver mines. While the Spanish royalty officially condemned slavery in the New World, the Indians were barely paid for their labor.

As deadly as swords or chains were the diseases introduced by the Europeans. The Inca had no resistance to measles, smallpox, and other viruses. About 40 percent of the Inca population was wiped out in epidemics spread by the Spaniards.

To this day, Pizarro is generally reviled in South America, as the strange story of a sculpture suggests. In the early 1930s, an artist carved a statue of a Spanish conquistador on a horse. He offered it to Mexico, claiming it was a likeness of Pizarro's cousin Cortés, the Spanish conqueror who defeated the Aztecs. The Mexicans refused the gift, not willing to glorify a man they considered a tyrant.

The artist then offered the sculpture to Peru. He told them that the statue was actually Pizarro. The Peruvians accepted it for a time. From 1934 to 2003, the statue stood in the middle of Lima. Finally, angry Peruvians demanded that it be removed. They refused to honor Pizarro, who they claimed was a mass murderer. Now the sculpture sits in a small park on the outskirts of town. Few visitors to the city ever see it.

Timeline of Terror

1200

1200: The Inca Empire begins around this time in Peru.

1440: The Inca expand their empire, which becomes known as the "four quarters of the world."

1469: Ferdinand and Isabella marry and begin unifying the Spanish kingdoms into one nation.

c. 1471: Francisco Pizarro is born in Trujillo, Spain. Historians disagree on the exact date of Pizarro's birth.

1492: Christopher Columbus discovers the New World.

1502: Pizarro leaves Spain for Hispaniola around this time.

1513: Pizarro is present when Vasco de Balboa becomes the first European to see the eastern rim of the Pacific Ocean.

1519: Hernán Cortés conquers the Aztecs in Mexico.

1524: Pizarro, along with Diego de Almagro, leads his first expedition to Peru, sailing along the Colombian coast.

1525–1527: Huayna Capac, the last great Inca emperor, dies around this time, and Inca civil war breaks out.

1528: Pizarro returns to Spain to secure King Charles's support for a final expedition.

1532: Pizarro defeats the Inca emperor Atahualpa at Cajamarca.

1533: Atahualpa is executed; Pizarro captures Cuzco, the Inca capital.

1535: Pizarro establishes the city of Lima.

1536–1537: The Spanish prevail in a six-month siege of Cuzco by the Inca emperor Manco.

1538: Pizarro and his brothers defeat Almagro in the Battle of Salinas. Almagro is executed.

1541: Pizarro is assassinated in Lima.

1541

GLOSSARY

allegiance (uh-LEE-junss) *noun* loyalty to someone or something

allure (a-LURE) *noun* the quality of being powerfully attractive

appease (uh-PEEZ) *verb* to make someone content or calm

archer (AR-chur) *noun* a person who uses a bow and arrow

balsa (BALL-suh) *noun* a very lightweight type of wood

brazier (BRAY-zhur) *noun* a pan for holding burning coals

cacique (kuh-SEEK) *noun* a native chief in Central and South America

captor (KAP-tur) *noun* someone who takes a person by force

caravel (CARE-uh-vel) *noun* a small sailing ship of the 1500s

cavalry (KAV-uhl-ree) *noun* soldiers who fight on horseback

chain mail (CHAYN MAYL) *noun* flexible armor made of interlinked metal rings

civilization (siv-il-uh-ZAY-shun) *noun* a highly developed and organized society

condor (KON-dur) *noun* a large vulture

conquest (KON-kwest) *noun* the act of defeating and taking control of an enemy

conquistador (kuhn-KEES-ta-door) *noun* a soldier in the Spanish conquest of the Americas

crossbow (KRAWSS-boh) *noun* a weapon that fires an armor-piercing bolt

descendant (di-SEND-uhnt) *noun* a person's child, grandchild, or other such relative on into the future

emperor (EM-pur-ur) *noun* the male ruler of an empire

empire (EM-pire) *noun* a group of regions that have the same ruler

123

harquebus (HAR-kwi-bis) *noun* a heavy but portable 15th-century gun

illegitimate (il-uh-JIT-uh-met) *adjective* born to a mother who is not legally married

indignant (in-DIG-nuhnt) *adjective* upset and annoyed out of a sense of unfairness

lance (LANSS) *noun* a long spear used by cavalry

loot (LOOT) *verb* to steal things during a riot or a war

maize (MAYZ) *noun* corn

mentor (MEN-tur) *noun* a trusted guide or teacher

native (NAY-tiv) *adjective* belonging to a place because one was born there

profane (pro-FAYN) *adjective* not concerned with religion

puppet (PUP-it) *noun* in politics, a leader whose actions are controlled by others

ransom (RAN-suhm) *noun* money or valuables that are demanded before someone who is being held captive can be set free

ruthlessness (ROOTH-lis-ness) *noun* the quality of being cruel and without pity

sacrifice (SAK-ruh-fise) *verb* to kill a person or an animal as an offering to a god

shackle (SHAK-uhl) *verb* to lock metal rings around the wrists or ankles of a prisoner

smallpox (SMAWL-poks) *noun* a very contagious and often fatal disease; it causes pimples that can leave permanent scars

spoils (SPOILZ) *noun* treasure taken from an enemy during war

vandal (VAN-duhl) *noun* someone who needlessly destroys other people's property

weevil (WEE-vuhl) *noun* a beetle that eats grain, fruit, and other crops

FIND OUT MORE

Here are some books and Web sites with more information about Francisco Pizarro and his times.

BOOKS

Calvert, Patricia. **The Ancient Inca (People of the Ancient World).** New York: Franklin Watts, 2005. (112 pages) *A beautifully illustrated book that explores the history, culture, and daily life of the Inca.*

Gruber, Beth. **National Geographic Investigates: Ancient Inca: Archaeology Unlocks the Secrets of the Inca's Past.** Washington DC: National Geographic Children's Books, 2007. (64 pages) *A fascinating look at how archeologists have worked to unlock the secrets of the Inca.*

Meltzer, Milton. **Francisco Pizarro: The Conquest of Peru.** New York: Marshall Cavendish, 2005. (80 pages) *An illustrated look at the life and explorations of Francisco Pizarro.*

Morrison, Marion. **Peru (Enchantment of the World, Second Series).** New York: Children's Press, 2000. (144 pages) *Describes the history, geography, and people of Peru.*

Somervill, Barbara. **Francisco Pizarro: Conquerer of the Incas.** Minneapolis: Compass Point Books, 2005. (112 pages) *A detailed account of how Pizarro journeyed to Peru and destroyed the Inca Empire.*

WEB SITES

http://encarta.msn.com/encyclopedia_761571358/pizarro_francisco.html
MSN Encarta's online encyclopedia article about Francisco Pizarro.

http://www.nationalgeographic.com/inca
National Geographic created this companion site for its fascinating series Inca Mummies: Secrets of a Lost World. *It includes an online documentary.*

http://www.pbs.org/conquistadors/index.html
This companion site to the PBS series Conquistadors *includes a section on the episode "Francisco Pizarro: The Conquest of the Incas."*

For Grolier subscribers:
http://go.grolier.com **searches:** Francisco Pizarro; Hernando Pizarro; Gonzalo Pizarro; Peru; Hispaniola; Ferdinand and Isabella

INDEX

AUTHOR'S NOTE AND BIBLIOGRAPHY

Francisco Pizarro was a ruthless soldier. He conquered an empire and destroyed a civilization—all for his own wealth and glory. He showed no mercy to his enemies. But seen in the light of his own time, Pizarro was probably no better or worse than other European conquerors—or even the Inca leaders he defeated.

As I wrote and researched this book, a lesson stuck with me: History changes. Sure, all the people in this book have been dead for hundreds of years; their stories can't change. But how we perceive them changes. There was a time when historians thought Pizarro and other conquistadors like Cortez were heroes—brave and bold adventurers. Those history books were mostly written by Europeans celebrating their conquests. But as time goes on, our view of history changes—as well as the historians telling the story. When Native American voices are heard, Pizarro's legacy becomes very different.

So who was Pizarro? A soldier? An adventurer? A murderer? History tells us that he was all of the above. But history also tells us that his story isn't over yet. Here are some of the sources I relied on in writing this book:

Gabai, Rafael Varon and Javier Flores Espinoza. **Francisco Pizarro and His Brothers: The Illusion of Power in Sixteenth-Century Peru**. Norman, OK: University of Oklahoma Press, 1997.

Hemming, John. **The Conquest of the Incas**. New York: Harvest/HBJ, 2003.

Manning, Ruth. **Francisco Pizarro**. Portsmouth, NH: Heinemann, 2001.

Stirling, Stuart. **Pizarro: Conqueror of the Inca**. Stroud, Gloucestershire, UK: Sutton Publishing, 2005.

Worth, Richard. **Pizarro and the Conquest of the Incan Empire in World History**. Berkeley Heights, NJ: Enslow Publishers, 2000.

—John DiConsiglio